Trees of Life

A PICTURESQUE JOURNEY

By Shelley Brienza

Photo by Shelley Brienza

Oh glorious tree,
How beautiful are thee?

Photo by Shelley Brienza

Schoharie Crossing-Yankee Hill Lock
Amsterdam, NY

North Adams, MA, Hillside Cemetery

Yaddo Gardens, Saratoga Springs, NY

Turning Stone Casino, Verona, NY

Author, Shelley Brienza
Olde Fort Hunter, NY

2020 Winter NYS

Historical Colonial Cemetery, Johnstown, NY

Historical Colonial Cemetery, Johnstown, NY

Historical Colonial Cemetery, Johnstown, NY

Beardslee Castle, Little Falls, NY

Beardslee Castle, Little Falls, NY

Beardslee Castle, Little Falls, NY

Beardslee Castle, Little Falls, NY

Schoharie Crossing-Yankee Hill Lock
Amsterdam, NY

Schoharie Crossing-Yankee Hill Lock
Amsterdam, NY

Schoharie Crossing-Yankee Hill Lock
Amsterdam, NY

Fulton, County, NY Winter 2019

Historical Colonial Cemetery, Johnstown, NY

Fulton County, NY Winter

Across the street from Beardslee Castle, Little Falls , NY

Fulton County, NY Winter 2020

Ice storm, Fulton County, NY 2020

Color photo, Beardslee Castle, original homestead, Little Falls, NY

Schoharie Crossing-Yankee Hill Park
Amsterdam, NY

Saratoga County Homestead
(Haunted asylum)
Middle Grove, NY

Tribes Hill, NY

Mason Lake, NY

Creepy

Nature's view through a windshield

Fulton County, NY

Colonial Cemetery, Johnstown, NY

The Great Sacandaga Lake, Northville, NY

Mayfield, NY

Sherman's Amusement Park
[abandoned]
Caroga Lake, NY

Broadalbin beach at night,
Broadalbin, NY

Sacandaga Lake, Northville, NY

Mason Lake, NY

Adirondack sunset, NY

Cemetery, Amsterdam, NY

Near Conklingville Dam, NY

Photo by S. Brienza

Beardslee Castle, Little Falls, NY

Snow covered cemetery

Sacandaga River, NY

Photo by S Brienza

North Pole, NY

Winter in the Northeast

Mountains of Mass.

Abandoned Sherman's Amusement Park
Caroga Lake, NY

Beardslee Castle, Little Falls, NY

Lock 12, Tribes Hill NY

Colonial Cemetery, Johnstown, NY
With Haunted in NY Founder,
Shelley Brienza

Olde Fort Hunter
Amsterdam, NY
Shelley Brienza

Canada Lake, NY

Colonial Cemetery, Johnstown, NY

Town of Mayfield, NY

Beardslee Castle property,
Little Falls, NY

I hope you have enjoyed taking a journey throughout the Mohawk Valley & beyond through the Life of Trees.

April 29, 2020
Photographer/Author
Shelley Brienza

No copies of photos may be used elsewhere